Grubbycup's Simple Hydroponics

The Path of the Garden Volume one: First steps.

D1523079

Grubbycup Stash

First Edition

Copyright © 2011 Grubbycup Stash

All rights reserved.

ISBN-13: 978-0615453521 (Grubbycup Seeds)

ISBN-10: 061545352X

Simple Hydroponics

Hydroponic systems can be both complicated and expensive, but they don't have to be. They can also be simple and elegant. The central concept of hydroponics is to garden using a rooting material that is not soil.

This booklet is intended for beginning gardeners. Some concepts have been simplified for easier comprehension.

Choosing a space for your indoor garden.

Closets, basements, spare rooms, and attics are all very common choices for a small to medium sized garden. Indoor gardens require both electricity and water, so keep distance from these resources in mind when choosing a location.

In order to be able to induce flowering, some plants have specific lighting schedule requirements. The garden may need to be lightproofed.

Once you have chosen the location of your garden, clean it. Many major indoor garden problems can be traced back to poor garden room hygiene. Besides, spills are much easier to clean up if the space was clean to start with.

This would also be a good time to figure out just how big of a mess it's going to be when the first spill happens. Spills will happen, it is a question of when and how much.

Remove any carpet if it is practical to do so.

Keep in mind that while you need to be able to tend to your plants, you may want to keep them in a location where guests won't trip over or disturb them.

For the inside walls the two most important things to keep in mind are reflectivity, and ease of cleaning. I prefer white, either a flat bathroom paint or plastic film. If you use a plastic film, make sure that there is enough clearance between the film and any heat source, such as your lights, to prevent it from getting too warm.

Make sure that you have sufficiently well grounded power for your lights and equipment. All electrical cords should have drip loops; the cord should have a loop near the outlet, so that if water is splashed on the cord, it will drip off before reaching the electrical outlet.

Especially if you are a private person, and would prefer that a fireman not visit your garden, do not use cheap extension cords or overload circuits. Any use of electricity should be kept as safe as possible.

TIP: Some indoor vegetables require hand pollination; others will broadcast pollen over a large area. Make sure you understand the life cycle of the plants you are growing.

Fluorescent Lighting

A fluorescent light is a sealed phosphor coated glass tube with a small bit of mercury and an inert gas. When current is applied, a portion of the mercury is excited until it turns from a liquid to a gas. The mercury gas gives off UV light, which is converted to visible light by the phosphor coating. If you break a bulb, be careful cleaning it up, don't breathe the fumes, and avoid skin contact with any part that may be contaminated with mercury.

It is possible to sprout, grow, and harvest under cheap shop lights (T12). The results won't be impressive, and you will likely want to move up to a better light, but it will supply enough light to prove the concepts. A few decades back they the most common artificial lighting for home indoor gardening.

Better quality fluorescent lighting has become much more available since then. T5 grow lights are a fair step up from the old T12s, and can be used to good effect.

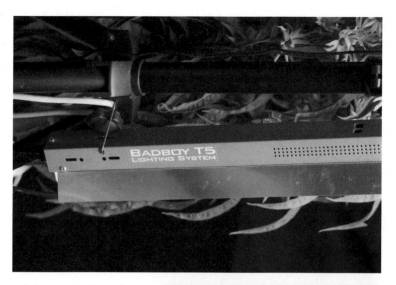

One of the major benefits of fluorescent lighting is that they don't produce a lot of intense waste heat to be dealt with. Since the operating temperature of the bulb is lower, the light can be placed closer to the canopy without heat stress.

Canopy management is important with fluorescent lighting, as the light from the row of several bulbs tends to form a flat plane.

Metal Halide (High Intensity Discharge)

Metal Halide (MH) makes use of some of the same basic principles as fluorescents. A variety of metal halides are added to the gas in the arc tube. The outer tube confines the UV, but allows the usable

light to pass. An additional phosphor coating is not needed.

Metal halides are often used for growth, either in conjunction with an HPS or by itself.

One benefit of metal halides that is not often mentioned, is that they are the most pleasant of the three to work under. They don't flicker like a fluorescent, and don't give an orange cast to everything like high pressure sodiums do.

However, the more pleasant light comes at a cost; metal halide lamps are less efficient than an equivalent HPS light by 10-15%.

High Pressure Sodium (High Intensity Discharge)

High pressure sodium (HPS) lights again use the same basic concept, but have a long cloudy arc bulb that contains metal sodium and mercury.

TIP: High pressure sodium and metal halide bulbs once hot must be allowed to cool before relighting.

High pressure sodium lights are most often used for flowering, either in conjunction with an MH or as the only light source. The light given off has an amber orange tint to it.

Ballasts

Make sure that the bulb and the ballast used to fire it match. A bulb fitting into the socket is no indication; you must check the wattage of the bulb to the output of the ballast. For example, only use a 400 watt bulb with a 400 watt ballast.

If using an older style coil ballast, they must also be matched to the type of bulb used. A 400 watt HPS bulb is fired with a 400 watt HPS ballast.

The newer digital ballasts can often fire either type as a feature, which can be very convenient, since you can purchase a MH bulb for growth and a HPS bulb for flowering with a single ballast.

Some digital ballasts even let you use different wattages, but make sure that's a feature that would be useful to you before purchasing one, as they tend to be more expensive.

Ballasts die, sooner or later; they wear out. Just in case its sooner, make sure your ballast is from a manufacturer with a good warranty, and make sure to keep the receipt and any other paperwork. Ballasts are expensive, and make sure you get the use out of it that you should.

If possible, keep the ballast iteself out of the garden environment, it's another source of waste heat to deal with.

Wattage

The higher the wattage, the greater the power consumption, and as a rule of thumb, the more heat they generate. The more waste heat that is generated, the stronger the need for cooling, and the further from the plants the lights have to be kept. A 60 watt T5 can be used without a light cooling system, and can be kept as close as a few centimeters away (although a light that close will need frequent adjusting as the plant gets taller). On the other end of the spectrum, a 1000 watt HID can cover a much larger area, but puts off heat in the ballpark of a small space heater, which can quickly cause heat damage to the canopy if the light is too close.

TIP: A pass through air cooled light hood will help you to vent the heat from the lamp before it heats the room.

As a quick test for heat, hold your hand out flat, with the back of your hand facing the light, and your palm facing the garden. By raising and lowering your hand you should feel a point where you can feel the heat with the hairs on the back of your hand, but your palm feels much cooler, that is the point of the maximum usable canopy height.

The size light you should get depends on the space you intend to garden.

Volt: The "pressure" or "potental difference". This difference in potential drives the electricity from one point to another.

Amp: The "flow amount". This is the "size of the pipe" the electricity travels.

Watt: Volts x Amps for a period of time. "Pressure" x "Flow amount". A small pipe under high pressure can transport the same amout as a large pipe under low pressure, so it's the combination of the two that determines the watts used.

Humidity

Low humidity requires more frequent watering, can exacerbate heat issues, and attract unwanted guests such as spider mites. High humidity is conducive to molds and mildews.

Temperature

Ideal temperatures are dependant on the type of plant being grown. Look up the particular climate needs of your plant, but between 21-29C (70-85F), is a good choice as a starting range for warm climate plants. Extended temperatures below 17C (63F) can cause some warm climate plants to go dormant. Growth also tends to stop at temperatures above 32C (90F) with some plants being more heat tolerant.

To keep your room temperature down you are better off venting the hot air than trying to dilute it. Hot air is just high energy air, and you are better off cooling a sealed pot of water by lifting the lid than adding ice cubes to keep it from boiling over.

Lights are likely to be the biggest heat source in your room. HID lights put out a lot of energy, and a fair part of that energy is expressed as heat. A vented pass through hood can quickly remove the heated air from the light before the heat passes too much of it's energy to the rest of the room. In an ideal situation, outside air is brought in through ductwork, passes through the hood, and is returned to the outside with a fan.

TIP: Solar powered fans can give an extra boost during the hottest part of the day without adding to your electric bill.

If the heat from the lights can be dealt with, then the ambient temperature of the room can be controlled with much less effort.

When designing any ducting, keep in mind that wide turns are better than sharp turns, and the hot air that you are trying to get rid of rises.

Try to draw air out of the room from the hottest air, and bring outside air in from the low/cool air .

The space itself needs air circulation as well, both to encourage evaporation, and to supply carbon dioxide. Plants absorb carbon dioxide(CO_2), and emit oxygen. Without some air movement this process can result in the plants sitting in a cloud of oxygen and not receiving enough carbon dioxide.

CO_2 is sometimes added to the environment artificially, although my preference is for the gardener, who is as much a part of the system as anything else, to spend time in the garden, and contribute your breath to the system. If you think that your garden isn't getting enough CO_2, bring a friend in and do some heavy breathing together.

In a garden, nothing good grows in stagnate water. Water from spills, watering, condensation etc. must have enough air circulation to dry out to maintain a healthy room. Water can move slowly, but it must be moving fast enough to stay oxygenated because once it goes stale it's a home for pathogens and bugs. The best defense against mold is to keep the air moving so it can't start.

A passive air vent may be required to replace the vented air (depending on how airtight the garden is). The incoming air should be taken from as cool a source as is available, and on the opposite side of the garden from the intake for the garden room vent.

Every situation is different, and in a small enough space, one fan may be able to accomplish more than one task.

Fans are rated in cubic feet per minute (CFM) or cubic meters per minute (CMM). Keep in mind, that just like with water pumps, the prominent number listed on the box is often how the device performs under a very light load.

It starts with a seed.

Whether purchased, gifted or gathered, quality harvests depend on quality seeds.

Seeds kept too wet may sprout prematurely. Seeds should be kept in a dry container at cool temperatures.

Sprouting Seeds

Before a seed will sprout, it must first be rehydrated.
To help with germination, an optional step is to soak seeds in water for 24 hours.

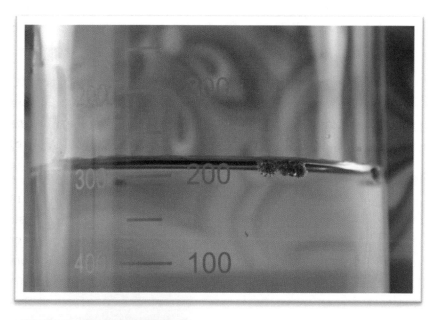

Another optional step is to moisten a paper towel, wring it out, and put it with the seeds in a plastic bag in a warm location to sprout.

If using this method, change the paper towel every few days to keep it fresh.

A crochet hook can be very handy as a probe, or to make a hole in media for a seed or cutting. With care it can even be used to seat sprouts in rockwool plugs.

Seeds may be planted directly into pots, or in starter cubes.

Starter cubes are made in a variety of materials.

Rockwool and coco plugs are common.

Inserts are available to allow seeds started in plugs to be kept neatly in standard 1020 trays.

Warm temperatures generally aid in germination.

Sometimes domes or plastic sheets are used to keep the humidity high while seeds sprout.

Many seeds can be sprouted by simply burying them 3 to 4 times their width, and kept moist, but not soggy, until sprouting.

TIP: There are many paths you can take to nurture a seed into sprouting, but starting with good seeds makes all of them easier.

Once the seeds have sprouted and have grown enough to become established, they should be transplanted into a larger container for growing.

Treat the roots gently while transplanting, as they are easily damaged.

Soil

When bringing plants that naturally grow outdoors, indoors, some choose to bring a little pocket of soil with them.

There are benefits to this: It buffers against changes, it has a very natural root support structure, and it is a familiar medium to many houseplant gardeners.

Growing in soil tends to be more forgiving of mistakes than growing in hydroponic gardens.

Soil is a very nice medium to start with, and teaches skills that come in handy if you decide to try hydroponics.

Some nutrients and mirconutirents are already present in soil.

Over time these starting nutrients are used up.

As the plant's root system replaces the media in the available space, adjusting the watering schedule to a more traditionally hydroponic one can mitigate some of the ill effects of becoming root-bound.

A plant growing naturally in the ground, that receives resources from its environment without human intervention is about as "soil" as you can get.

In nature, air, nutrients and water needs are either naturally occurring, or the plant dies.

One advantage to human intervention, is that if one of the requirements is not naturally present, it can be added to the system, which dramatically expands the range of possible planting locations.

A passive hydroponic system is similar to growing in soil, and can help you learn how to manage hydroponic watering and nutrition needs.

Consider trying out a bag of hydroponic media and some hydroponic nutrients in a hand watered pot to see if you like it.

With an air pump and/or a water pump, you can turn a passive system into an active one.

Hydroponic Media

Inert hydroponic media, such as perlite, rockwool, clay or coco, does not contain nutrients .

The root system must have access to both air and water. Similar to a human throat, too much water and too little air causes drowning, too much air and too little water causes dehydration. In both cases, slight dehydration is a less traumatic experience than a slight drowning. While you are adjusting the watering schedule, erring too dry is better than erring too wet.

Lightweight Expanded Clay Aggregate (LECA)

LECA is clay that has been heated to expand and solidify. It is extremely airy, and well suited for systems that have over watering issues. It is not well suited for sprouting, and may float if flooded. It is reusable after washing with a dilute sterilizing solution and then rinsing.

Coco Fiber (Coir)

Coco fiber is made from coconut husks. Care should be taken to either rinse coir or buy pre-rinsed. It is more like growing in soil than most other choices.

Coir breaks down over time, and is not very reusable in comparison to some other choices.

Rockwool

Rockwool is heated basalt spun like fiberglass or cotton candy. It can be an irritant when dry, and can make small itchy cuts in skin (similar to fiberglass). It sometimes is basic (high pH) when

new, if so rinse with a light acid such as lemon juice before use.

It is less prone to overwatering than coir, but more than perlite or LECA. It retains water well, and is not very reusable

None

There are hydroponic systems that use little to no media to hold the root structure. Deep water culture, aeroponic, and nutrient film do not rely heavily on media.

Vermiculite

Vermiculite is heated at high temperatures where the moisture it contains expands to "puff". Dry vermiculite is dusty and may irritate, so precautions should be taken to limit exposure. Vermiculite compacts and breaks down over repeated use. It is very airy, and is often used to lighten mixes.

Perlite

Perlite makes for a nice medium to use in a simple passive system.

Perlite has been heated at high temperatures to turn internal moisture into steam in order to expand it.

Dry perlite can be a dust hazard, and care should be taken not to breathe in the particles. Wet and rinse new product before use.

Perlite is extremely airy, and is difficult to overwater.

However it also does not retain water well, so frequent watering is needed. Dry perlite floats, and as such is unsuitable for some methods. It can be rinsed and reused many times. Perlite is my personal favorite grow medium.

Passive Hydroponics

The simplest hydroponic systems are passive. The media containing the plant is watered by an unpowered force such as capillary action.

A pot filled with perlite in a tray with solution in the bottom is an example of passive hydroponics, and is a good choice for a first method to try.

Either a wick is used to transport solution, or the media itself is kept wet enough with nutrient solution to remain hydrated.

By leaving some solution in the bottom of a tray the plant can stay hydrated.

To prevent the solution from going stale, only a day or two's worth of nutrient water should be added to the bottom of the tray, and the media should occasionally be allowed to slightly dry before adding more solution, especially in humid conditions.

Most hand watered systems use some variation of this principle.

Although the principle uses capillary action to draw the solution to the plant roots, water the top of the media at least occasionally.

All you need to try passive hydroponics is a tray, a pot, a little media, some hydroponic fertilizer, light, water, and a seed. Add a little love and care, and you are well on your way.

Active Hydroponics.

Active hydroponics use some sort of powered air or water pump to move the nutrient solution to the roots.

Drip

In a drip system nutrient solution is pumped to low volume drip emitters under pressure, or the solution is pumped to an elevated reservoir, and gravity feeds the emitters.

> In drip systems, nutrient solution is dripped from low volume emitters over a long period of time.

Aeration of the solution is controlled by the media used, how much the media is allowed to dry between waterings, and amount (if any) of air added to the solution while in the reservoir.

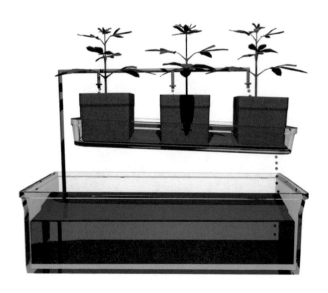

Here is a variation where a second reservoir tank has been added.

The lower reservoir has the pump and the return.

A line from the upper reservoir supplies the drip emitters.

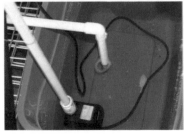

Nutrient Film Technique (NFT)

In a nutrient film system the roots are constantly exposed to a thin film of aerated nutrient, or a porous mat is continuously soaked with nutrient. .

In the example to the right, this plant receives its fluid from a thin layer of water going over a small fall.

NFT: A low volume of nutrient solution is continuously applied to the roots.

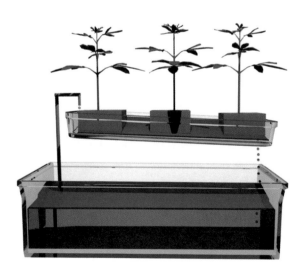

Ebb and Flow

In an ebb and flow system, the pots are placed in a tray, and the solution is pumped from a reservoir into the tray to flood it. This waters the media, then the solution is allowed to drain back into the reservoir. A timer controls how often the tray is flooded.

> Ebb and Flow: Floods the roots in the nutrient solution which is then removed to allow respiration.

A well aerated solution will help buffer minor over watering.

Deep Water Culture (DWC)

> DWC: A high volume of aerated nutrient solution is continuously available to the lower portion of the root system

A DWC system can be as simple as adding an airline to the nutrient solution for aeration. These simple systems are sometimes referred to as "bubblers". The plant is suspended above the nutrient solution, and the roots are allowed to dangle down.

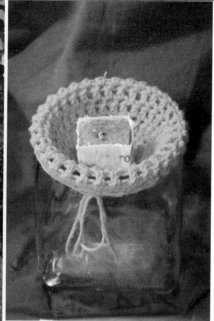

One form of deep water culture uses a movable raft that floats on the surface of the tank.

As long as the plant's needs are being met, they can do well under a variety of conditions.

At the extreme end of aeration are the aeroponic systems.

Aeronic

Aeroponic systems use the same basic principles as a DWC, but instead of adding air to the solution, solution spray is added to the air for the roots to absorb.

> Aeroponic: Small liquid solution particles are continuously applied to freestanding roots.

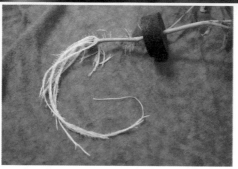

Nutrients

Water

While not technically a nutrient, but the transport agent for nutrients, water is an important requirement for growing healthy plants. Slight under watering is less detrimental than slight over watering, so if in doubt, run towards the dry side. The quality of the end solution is in part determined by the quality of the initial water used for the base liquid.

Plant Food

As with water, too little is easier to recover from than too much. The three main components of a balanced meal for your plants are: the macronutrients, micronutrients, and additives.

Macronutrients - NPK

Nitrogen(N), phosphorus(P), and potassium(K) are the three macronutrients. They are the most important nutritionally to the plant, and therefore should be the most important to you. The percentage by weight of each can be identified by reading the three numbers listed on a fertilizer. So for instance, a fertilizer listed as 20-10-10 is 20 percent nitrogen, 10 percent phosphorus, 10 percent potassium, and 60 percent something else.

During vegetative growth, more nitrogen is used by the plants, so more nitrogen should be used in the solution. A fertilizer that has the first number higher than the other two.

During flowering, nitrogen use is decreased, phosphorus and potassium use is increased, so more phosphorus and potassium should be used. Therefore, a plant food with a lower first number (but higher than zero) is desired.

Nitrogen

Nitrogen is used in the creation and use of chlorophyll and photosynthesis. Chlorophyll gives the leaves their green color. Too little and the older leaves turn pale green, then yellow, then die. Too much and the leaves turn dark 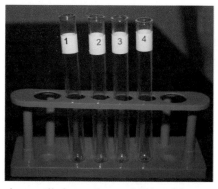 green, stems turn rigid, and the plant will show signs of ill health. More nitrogen is used in the vegetative grow phase, when photosynthesis activity is at its peak, but some is required throughout the adult life of the plant since photosynthesis is always needed by the plant.

Phosphorus

Phosphorus deficiency is not an as easily noticeable problem as a nitrogen deficiency. The plants will often only display it by underperforming. To be on the safe side, add more phosphorous during flowering to encourage flower development.

Potassium

Potassium is used in the "plumbing" of the plant: liquid movement within the plant, stems, roots etc. It is also used in photosynthesis. Potassium deficiency often shows as a yellowing/dying of the leaf edges, curled under leaves, followed by spots in the interior of the leaf face.

Micronutrients

The major difference between soil and hydroponic growing is the source of the micronutrients. In a traditional soil garden, the micronutrients are already present in the media (soil). As a result, many soil fertilizers only address the macronutrient (N-P-K) requirements. Since hydroponic systems use a sterile media without micronutrients, they must be added to the system. Nutrients used in hydroponic systems should address these micronutrient needs, or a micronutrient additive should be used.

Testing the solution

pH is a scale from 1 (most acidic) to 14 (most basic) with neutral at 7. The ideal range depends on the type of plant grown. 6.0-6.2 is a fair estimate. If you are within a half point or so, don't try to adjust it. Adjustments are made by adding the opposite. If the solution has a pH value too low (is acidic), add a base to raise the pH. If the solution is too basic (pH too high), an acid is added to lower it. If your pH is not in this range, too basic is more forgiving than too acidic.

The ppm or EC value for the solution, gives a rough idea of the total conductivity of substances in the nutrient solution, but it does not give the specific N-P-K values. The information gathered with a meter must be coupled with the specific nutritional needs of the plant.

Sometimes water is best

Just like people, plants use more water when they are hot to help cool themselves. During periods of high temperatures, add plain fresh water to prevent overfeeding during these periods of heavy liquid use by the plants.

Other additives

Other useful hydroponic additives are not nutritional in nature
 Some are mixed with the nutrient solution to adjust pH, by either adding an acid to a solution that is too basic, or a base if the solution is too acidic.

Mycorrhizae are a naturally occurring root fungus. Spores are sometimes added to help establish colonies in hydroponic systems.

There are many different nutrients and additives on the market. Before purchasing, find out what benefits each offers to your plants.

Thank you

Thank you for taking the time to read this booklet. The path of gardening can be very therapeutic, for both body and mind. Best wishes to you.

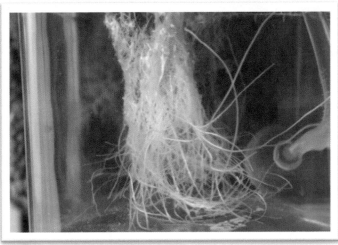

Gardens should grow both the plants, and the gardener

About the author:

Why Grubbycup?

Imagine that your "to do" list for the day includes changing the oil in the car, re-staining the deck chairs out back, and turning over your compost pile. All of this is hard, dirty, thirsty work, so you fix yourself a beverage to take with you. Do you take one of the fine cut crystal wine goblets with you? No, of course not. You take that beat up oddball glass that doesn't go with anything, and you go get the work done. That glass is a grubby cup.

I have had the good fortune to have had gardening articles printed around the globe, and translated into languages I myself cannot speak. For this I am grateful to you, my gentle readers.

Gardening is a set of skills, and if you decide to, you can learn those skills and garden.

This booklet is an attempt to help you.

Peace, love, and puka shells,
Grubbycup.

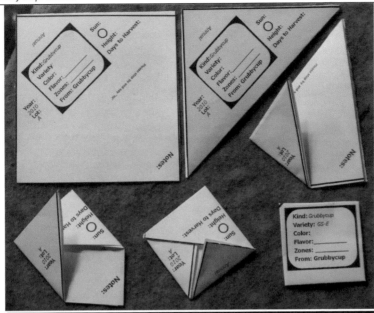

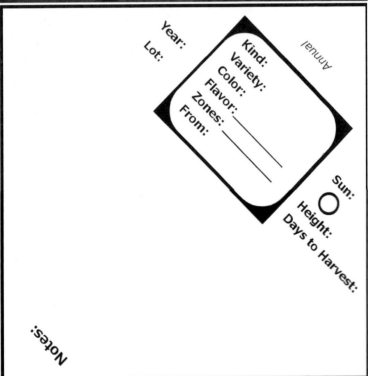

10367114R0

Made in the USA
Lexington, KY
26 July 2011